CLASS

First published 2021 by order of the Tate Trustees
by Tate Publishing, a division of Tate Enterprises Ltd,
Millbank, London SW1P 4RG
www.tate.org.uk/publishing

A catalogue record for this book is available from the British Library
ISBN 978 1 84976775 0

Distributed in the United States and Canada by ABRAMS, New York

Library of Congress Control Number applied for

Senior Editor: Alice Chasey
Series Editors: Mels Evers and James Finch
Production: Juliette Dupire
Picture Researcher: Roz Hill
Designed by Narrate + Kelly Barrow
Colour reproduction by DL Imaging, London
Printed in Wales by Cambrian Printers

Front cover: Henry Robert Morland, *A Laundry Maid Ironing* 1765–82
(see.p.37)

Measurements of artworks are given in centimetres, height before width,
before depth.

CLASS

NATHALIE OLAH

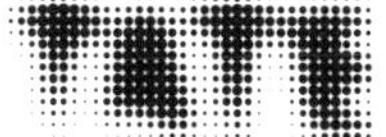

Director's Statement

'Look Again' is a bold new publishing programme from Tate Publishing and Tate Britain. In twelve books, published in three stages, we are providing a platform for some of the most exciting contemporary voices writing today to explore the national collection of British art in their own way, and reconnect art to our lives today. The books have been developed ahead of the rehang of Tate Britain's collection, which will be launched in 2023 and will foreground many of the artworks discussed here. In these first four texts – *Gender* by Travis Alabanza, *Feminism* by Bernardine Evaristo, *Empire* by Afua Hirsch, and *Class* by Nathalie Olah – we are offered unique perspectives on a wide range of artworks across British history, and encouraged to look closely, and to look again.

Alex Farquharson, Director, Tate Britain

In the foreground of J.M.W. Turner's *Ploughing Up Turnips, near Slough (Windsor)* – a painting first exhibited in 1809 and showcasing scenes of husbandry on the border between Berkshire and Buckinghamshire – a black cow nuzzles the day's harvest, snooping around for a snack (see p.33). Its master, an overseer of labour in King George III's new agrarian economy, turns his back, distracted by the flurry of activity implied by the workers' imprecise outlines which blend seamlessly with the peaty landscape that extends all around. The labourers are working, but not on the task at hand, a surplus of produce strewn and scattered along the ground.

The scene is one of human frailty and fallibility, of the tiny spectacle of the farmhand in an age of encroaching mechanisation and industrial revolution. The fact that cows would be trusted where men and women would not, gleaming hides humiliating the tatty get-up of the peasants who variously tend to broken ploughs, nurse their young and scrub at the root vegetables, tells us everything we need to know about the value being ascribed to human life under such conditions. But it is also a painting that comments on the evolving terrain of property and wealth extraction, following Britain's adoption of an enclosure model that divided up and privatised the common land. In the background and on the horizon, Windsor Castle (centre) and Eton

College (right) both stand with a stolid permanence. Landlords in their own right, but also broods of the land-owning class, their shadowy spectre is at once ominous and serene, belonging to a world of far more leisurely proportions than the one depicted in high resolution.

As the critic Michelle Miller explains, 'The transition from subsistence farming to more intense, market-driven agriculture made possible by enclosures left great numbers entirely dependent on wage labor and placed them increasingly under the control of the landowners and farmers who hired them.' Turnips were a known symbol of enclosed farming, supporting a mixed style of agriculture only possible via this method, through the provision of both their root – a crop   and their leaves, which served to sustain grazing cattle. The sombre atmosphere of Turner's painting, then, offers a comment on the falsity of this apparent progress, and the ruinous and also wasteful effects of accelerated production, as well as a looming foreboding of latter-day rentier capitalism.

The story of class is the story of our relationship to labour and capital. This incontrovertible point has become contentious in recent years, however, as class consciousness has been eroded through the creation of more disparate types of work, as well as the promotion of individualism. It was Margaret

Thatcher's masterstroke to impose the controversial Right to Buy scheme in the UK in the 1980s, thereby creating a generation of homeowners whose existence would confound the traditional class hierarchies. But this confusion was also caused across the Western world by the erosion of industry, its replacement by a service-based economy, and the opening up of university education. Those in power would now claim that we lived in a 'classless society': the truth, far from it, was that while inequality was still rife, it would now be that much harder to identify and to organise along economic lines.

As a result, we have seen fierce debates arise between those arguing for a definition of class that encompasses accent, regional identity and education level – factors that contribute towards a person's 'cultural capital' – and those loyal to a more material reading, focused solely on wealth and income. Class can never be separated from questions of capital, but one's ability to accrue capital and ascend through the class system, which in a neoliberal society is the only guarantee of security, certainly can be influenced by cultural factors. In this climate, where it is incumbent on each of us to distinguish ourselves in order to boost our employability, the arts – knowledge of, proximity to and participation in – become a weapon, used in the promotion of some and the punishment of others. The question of who gets to consume and create art is one that is intimately tied up in notions of class, as is the question of who gets to decree certain cultural artefacts worthy of our attention. Knowledge of fine art, literature, music and theatre will grant certain advantages in a professional setting, be it a job interview, university application process or after-work drinks. Of course, there is nothing inherently prohibitive to working people in understanding these ideas or subjects – quite the opposite – but for the fact of being time-poor and unable to devote several hours a week to reading Proust.

Only by coming to understand art's role as a cultural *product* in this sense, with a political and economic life, are we able to untangle its place in a complex set of neoliberal conditions that underscore the class system as we currently know it. Such an analysis does not have to come at the expense of more aesthetic, philosophic or emotional considerations, and neither does it strip the artwork of its essential magic or intrigue. But it is the point of this essay to show that by adding a class dimension to our thinking, we can magnify the significance of certain works and open ourselves up to whole new ways of seeing.

In the case of *Ploughing Up Turnips*, that means transforming our perception to see the shrewd social commentary in an otherwise quiet and unassuming landscape. Where other contemporary or near-contemporary portrayals of agriculture painted a bucolic scene of joyful participation and pageantry, Turner's seems to choke under a sickly yellow light, its challenge to the supposedly advanced developments taking place in agriculture expressed quietly through a set of visual cues. Throughout Turner's work, miasmic scenes heralded the arrival of industrial smog, but also carried a dirge for the social ills that attended such smog – the growing inequality and erosion of human sovereignty taking place as a result of industrial transformation and the expansion of empire. Turner's landscapes are far more uncanny than those produced in the years prior to his arrival on the art scene. Satisfied with offering the viewer a spectacle of apparent peace and prosperity were artists such as George Stubbs and Thomas Gainsborough, whose more crystalline renditions of the farming industry included verdant pastures, calm blue skies, and clouds flecked with an optimistic pink light.

In Stubbs's *Haymakers* and *Reapers* 1785, nature itself becomes more compliant than in reality – hay forming neat, fluffy bundles, and the workers' clothes not yet besmirched by mud or sweat (see p.35). Though painted before the imposition of the Inclosure Act, these paintings serve as an alibi for an agricultural industry that was nevertheless

"ONLY BY COMING TO UNDERSTAND ART'S ROLE AS A CULTURAL *PRODUCT* ..., WITH A POLITICAL AND ECONOMIC LIFE, ARE WE ABLE TO UNTANGLE ITS PLACE IN A COMPLEX SET OF NEOLIBERAL CONDITIONS THAT UNDERSCORE THE CLASS SYSTEM AS WE CURRENTLY KNOW IT. "

making increased demands on its workers in the late eighteenth century. Best known for its sleek, cinematic renderings of noble steeds and their wealthy owners, much of Stubbs's work was commissioned by wealthy patrons and intended for a similar audience.

But there is a reminder in his landscapes and collective portraits of a trend in more recent years, too, for advertisements centred on the spectacle of the jubilant worker. In 2019, for example, and after countless reports of its employees being monitored to the point of not being allowed to use the toilet[1], a certain home delivery service issued a Christmas TV ad campaign complete with jolly lorry driver belting out the 1960s pop song 'Everybody Needs

[1] See the *Guardian*, 26 March 2021, www.theguardian.com/technology /2021/mar/25/amazon-delivery-workers-bathrooms-memo

Somebody to Love'. No different to the advertising agencies employed in the service of large corporations in the twenty-first century, then, many artists of the late eighteenth and early nineteenth centuries worked in the service of benefactors who were keen to put a more wholesome spin on their degrading cultivation and harvesting practices.

This tendency also went beyond applying a jolly veneer to the drudgery of farming, to creating a whole new stock of characters, cartoonish in their proportions and tasked with assuaging the guilt of the British class system. These characters, not unlike the noble savage of eighteenth- and nineteenth-century novels, were the recipients of an honourable poverty, one that conferred a privilege or a holiness on its subjects, thereby eliminating the possibility of critiquing the social conditions that had led to its existence. The subjects of this honourable poverty thrived under the glow of their delicate perspiration. In Henry Robert Morland's *A Laundry Maid Ironing* c.1765–82, the almost iridescent skin of a worker – miraculously protected from the sun's harsh rays since birth – is matched only by the sculptural sheen of her coiffed hair and perfectly polished implements (see p.37). She irons serenely, a grateful reverie falling over a face that smiles vacantly at a piece of cloth. Likewise, in Thomas Gainsborough's *The Housemaid* c.1782–6, a woman stands poised and luminescent on the doorstep of her workplace (see p.38). While only a sketch, we see the ambition to depict a radiant form, contrasted against the rather more slipshod dimensions of her immediate setting, complete with strewn tools, wonky steps and weeds.

In both cases, the transformation of labour into something of a lifestyle choice is clear from the women's flimsy grip on their implements, perhaps the clearest indication of the scenes' artificial staging. These are props, objects dislocated from their function and repurposed as hollow symbols in portrayals whose lack of credibility verges on the burlesque. In the spirit of what is now popularly termed 'cos-play', artists such as Gainsborough were known to model their working-class subjects on sitters of a higher social standing, mimicking a trend also common at contemporary masquerades and balls. It is speculated that *The Housemaid* is a sketch of the aristocratic Mrs Graham in working-class costume, daughter of the 9th Lord Cathcart (Ambassador to Catherine the Great). From the sentiment of these paintings, then, down to the very practical dynamics of their creation, solidarity with the working class remained virtual, tokenistic, and, in many cases, a game.

In this eighteenth-century version of shabby chic – that is, a confected view of poverty, shown through the voyeuristic gaze of the middle and upper classes – the artist also seems incapable of resisting the urge to sexualise and objectify. Female subjects assume a posture of submission – the coy, downward or far-away glance and vacant smile as distant from the confident and direct stare of most noble portraiture as is possible to imagine. As suggested by the title, *A Laundry Maid Ironing* constitutes a 'type' rather than a portrait of a given sitter, demonstrating the anonymity and interchangeability of working-class subjects who would only ever be depicted in the performance of some task. Meanwhile, the complexions of these working-class types seem to have been overlaid with a gauzy filter, making their outlines nebulous and blurry. The sovereignty of the body melts away before our very eyes, rendering the subject compliant and powerless; rather than comprising a whole, sentient being with the suggestion of a rich inner life, these vague signifiers of womanhood become little more than the property of the viewer.

Likewise, and in another scene of sentimentalised struggle, the figure of a peasant becomes desaturated and ghost-like under the garish blaze of colour emanating from two child philanthropists, in a painting by the portrait artist William Beechey (see p.39). The scene recalls the parable of the Good Samaritan, projecting a pious quality onto the two young heirs, whose disembodied heads, placed atop a pair of wings, might easily pass for Renaissance cherubs. These children are identified as the offspring of fourth-generation plantation owner Francis Ford, and despite the shadowy bower under which they stand, a spotlight directs our gaze towards their biblical act of generosity.

In a modern context, Beechey's painting might be considered 'poverty porn', the term given to cynical depictions of hardship aimed at soliciting an intense, emotional reaction. This almost libidinal need to take pity on the poor, but also to use the image of poverty to vindicate the rich and influential, has led to the creation in more recent years of celebrity charity drives in developing countries, as well as the farce of rich patrons visiting charities in urban centres up and down the country. For centuries, the spectacle of the benevolent lord or lady has been used to obfuscate and distract from the origins and causes of class inequality, a Christian sanctimony absolving these figures of their role in a wider system of exploitation and ruin. Beechey's painting unwittingly lays bare – and makes more obvious – the dynamic by which a deliberate attempt to highlight the goodness of a generous benefactor ends up denigrating and humiliating the recipient.

We are only able to make these observations now – about the obvious deception in the

"FOR CENTURIES, THE SPECTACLE OF THE BENEVOLENT LORD OR LADY HAS BEEN USED TO OBFUSCATE AND DISTRACT FROM THE ORIGINS AND CAUSES OF CLASS INEQUALITY."

advertising techniques employed by the tech industry, or the latent hypocrisy in TV charity drives – thanks to the effort of a great many artists, writers and thinkers whose work has opened our eyes to the often insidious ways in which power exerts itself. One such writer was Roland Barthes, whose 1957 essay collection *Mythologies* considered several, seemingly inconsequential aspects of popular culture, looking at their role in the maintenance and perpetuation of certain power struggles and systems of control – a process he termed 'naturalisation'. While there is nothing inevitable about these systems, the ruling class is invested in a contrary narrative, one that often asserts its rightful existence and dominance. Certain works reinforce this naturalisation, while it has been those that challenged its fundamental absurdity and falsehood that have staked the course of art history throughout the late nineteenth and early twentieth centuries, developing one of art's main functions as a force of antagonism in late capitalist societies.

This evolution is complex, of course, and not without its many meanderings, internal contradictions and counter-examples. Since the early twentieth century, for example, there has been a counter-current that embraces the commodity value of art, whose adherents have, to varying degrees of sincerity, played with the boundaries between art and commerce. It is a strain that is arguably winning in the present moment, with hundreds of artists sitting atop multi-million-dollar fortunes, and as a struggle ensues for the soul of the art world between collectors creating new ways to privatise and trade, through innovations such as NFTs, and those seeking to democratise, open up and make work accessible to all.

Nevertheless, one of the dominant modalities of twentieth-century art was the interrogation of capital's dominion over modern life. From Dadaism with its mocking of the art world and its market-driven turn, to social realism and its confronting images of everyday drudgery, several artists, spanning many genres, concerned themselves with the profit motive and its necessary creation of new forms of exploitation. What Turner implied, through the Trojan horse of his select landscapes, was made explicit by excoriating modernists and postmodernists working a century later.

Jacob Epstein was an avant-garde pioneer of modernist sculpture, whose work encompassed an eclectic mix of styles. One of his early works, a now-disfigured sculpture simply titled *Torso in Metal*, serves as a simulacrum of modernist antipathy and the dawning realisation that machinery might not be the solution to society's ills as once imagined, being harnessed instead by those in power to supply new methods of destruction (see p.40). Originally placing the work atop a rock drill, in an almost deferential gesture to the machine, Epstein – following the rapid technological developments made during the First World War that led to more than 40 million, mostly working-class deaths – later removed the implement, as well as severing the figure at the torso and removing the left hand and right forearm. The sculpture's trajectory, then, from a towering spectacle of possibility to a cowed figure bashfully deflecting our gaze, is a symbol of the shame of this event and its wider implications for the future of mankind.

This echoed a general cynicism and resistance towards the machine that was taking place

"... COMPARED TO THE AMERICAN AND CONTINENTAL EUROPEAN TRADITIONS, BRITAIN ONLY MADE A SMALL CONTRIBUTION TO ART DEPICTING THE EVERYDAY CONDITIONS OF THE WORKING CLASSES ... IN THE TWENTIETH CENTURY."

throughout the late nineteenth and early twentieth centuries. If enclosed farming had made workers more reliant on landowners, then the industrial revolution – up to and including the creation of the automotive industry by Henry Ford – had done the same to manufacturing, making workers dependent on the factory owner and industrialist. Yet compared to the American and Continental European traditions, Britain only made a small contribution to art depicting the everyday conditions of the working classes (see 'social realism') in the twentieth century. L.S. Lowry is perhaps the most famous chronicler, his landscapes showcasing a populace engulfed and made minuscule, anonymous and unknowable by the expansion of industry, but other modernists, too, such as Henry Moore and (the now disgraced) Eric Gill, made a contribution in their occasional depictions of labour, though more frequently in their transmutations of man under industrial conditions into a hardened form made of reinforced materials. Moore and Barbara Hepworth deserve mention for their services to the cause of public art, which sought to democratise and give back to communities artworks that would otherwise have been consigned to the paywall of the gallery. Moore's *Family Group*, while traditional by today's standards, broke with the archetype of collective noble portraiture to showcase a version of family life that was less sentimental, more practical: the family of the working man in all its sturdy, resolute and protective power. Meanwhile, *The Deluge* 1920 by Winifred Knights carries a similar, ominous foreboding of technology's effect on society to Epstein's *Torso*, with its haunting reference to the biblical flood. Incorporating figures whose bodies carry the curved shape of weariness and toil, the scene recalls Knights's experiences witnessing the detonation of a TNT plant, but the painting's spectacle of human submission in the face of brute force was all the more relevant owing to the recent fact of war.

In the post-Fordist society of the late twentieth century, however, communication technology had paved the way for the corporation, whose *modus operandi* was in commandeering of the worker's *time*. Today, most of us are paid to attend our workplace for a designated number of hours, rather than the delivery of a specific quantity of goods. Labour in the middle of the twentieth century had largely shifted to a model of attendance, then, where additional pay could only be sought through the further erosion of an individual's free time and privacy (this is complicated further by the emergence in more recent years of the gig economy and low-paid services, where pay can, and often is, docked according to 'poor performance').

Interrogating the idea of time and its luxury status in a society that makes increased demands on people to work longer hours and devote more of 'themselves' to their jobs, the contemporary artist Ruth Ewan created *We could have been anything we wanted to be (red version)* 2011, adapting the usual function of a clock, and dividing the day into ten hours of a hundred minutes each (and each minute into a hundred seconds), to create a device that mimicked the measurements of the decimal French Republican Calendar (see p.41). Implemented after the French Revolution, for thirteen years the French Republic operated by an independent system of timekeeping divorced from the rest of the world. Ewan's work is a comment on the arbitrary nature of a system that nevertheless governs our lives, as well as a melancholic nod to the ambitions of the revolution and its dream of equality and prosperity for all. The revolutionaries could scarcely have anticipated the clocking-in and clocking-out system of the twentieth century, or its latter-day equivalent, the perpetual green light of attendance on Zoom or Teams, but their act of defiance demonstrated the abstract nature of time, with Ewan making the challenge that we could have therefore chosen to relate to it in ways that better served our needs.

The fact of being time-poor is at the heart of this work, which asks: what could we do, who could we be, and what imaginary potential might we unlock by releasing the vast majority of people from the tyranny of the working day? The title of the work, taken from the 1976 musical comedy *Bugsy Malone*, contains nostalgia for an unrealised future, where all of society might experience the freedoms of creativity and self-determination.

Marx's theory of alienation, made clear here through Ewan's work, suggested that the vast majority of people are prevented from achieving agency over their lives due to their subjugation to the profit motive of the capitalist. But it is also the idea that modern production methods have led to the worker becoming increasingly detached from the fruits of their labour. At the time Marx was writing *Capital*, a growing number of people were becoming concerned with the psychic impact of becoming a cog in the machine, and the erosion of a fundamental aspect of the human experience, as well as a cornerstone of mental wellbeing, that was taking place as a result of never seeing, touching or being involved – beyond a small, abstracted contribution – to the creation of a given product or service.

That being the case, the artist, by contrast, exists as one of the few privileged exceptions, overseeing their work from start to finish. But is this a reality? Part of the illusion of the artist as a doyen or demigod stems from their ability to transcend the mechanics of the labour model, to represent a form of *unalienated* labour that eludes the vast majority of people. This economic factor contributes as much to the artist's mythic status and appeal as any romantic notion of creativity and unfettered imagination. But this summation of the artist's duties is only partially true, and as art came to deal more and more in questions of labour, production and the distribution of wealth throughout the twentieth century, it would also need to address its own internal relationship to these dynamics, as well as its own role in a system of commodity-making and profiteering. The myth of the lone genius has often been used to conceal the art world's own exploitative tendencies and biases, as well as the *collective* effort that has often gone into creating a given work. In this sense, the artist who takes final credit (and the lion's share of the pay) is no different to the landowner or industrialist, extracting vast quantities of wealth from other people's labour. This is even used in defence of artists who flagrantly embrace commerce, such as Andy Warhol, creator among other things of the world-famous 'Factory': that they are simply being more candid about the commercial and exploitative tendencies of their industry.

The Pre-Raphaelite Brotherhood was an early effort to redress this dynamic. Two founding members, William Holman Hunt and John Everett Millais, had attended the Chartist gathering on parliament, with its demands for workers' rights, while the third, Dante Gabriel Rossetti, was the son of an Italian revolutionary. Their formation as a collective was itself a rejection of the individualistic ambition that had only been compounded in an age of industry, but the group also sought to elevate artisanal methods above the commercial modes of production, championing the skill of the craftsperson in work that bore the markings of the human hand. An emphasis on greater equality included the use of working-class models known to the artists and whose own creative practices were nurtured and cultivated by the group.

The group was also closely linked to poet, novelist, textile designer, print maker and campaigner William Morris, whose many achievements included the founding of Morris, Marshall, Faulkner & Co., along with Rossetti and Edward Burne-Jones, among others (see p.42). Together they decorated Victorian Britain with hand-drawn repeat patterns scaled through production methods, some very old, that brought the craftsperson closer to their materials than in mass-produced circumstances, reinstating indigo dyeing and the fine arts of tapestry and carpet weaving. The ambition to bring fine art into every home was later recognised in the 1920s, when founder of the Bauhaus Walter Gropius acknowledged his indebtedness to the work of Morris and John Ruskin – the Bauhaus remaining arguably the most ambitious attempt in Western history to democratise art and design for the practical enhancement of people's everyday lives.

From the well-meaning and pragmatic at the end of the nineteenth century to the more scornful gaze of much contemporary art: *Set Sail for the Levant: A Board Game About Debt (or a Social Satire)* 2007 by Olivia Plender is a work of resistance that cleaves open the pervasive realism of late capitalism – the realism affected through Barthes' naturalisation – to simplify and make plain

"THE MYTH OF THE LONE GENIUS HAS OFTEN BEEN USED TO CONCEAL THE ART WORLD'S OWN EXPLOITATIVE TENDENCIES AND BIASES, AS WELL AS THE *COLLECTIVE* EFFORT THAT HAS OFTEN GONE INTO CREATING A GIVEN WORK."

the ills of the global debt crisis (see p.44). Mimicking the dynamics that keep the Global South perpetually impoverished and beholden to the North, but also the dynamics of all debt and the plight of all workers prevented from achieving agency and self-determination, the game's rules contain one fundamental flaw: no one can ever win. Much like the manual labourers in Turner's painting outside of Windsor, the participants in Plender's game are operating in a rigged system of extraction, profiteering and inheritance. Wealth will forever be ensconced in palaces of privilege and power, while the working person – fast made obsolete in an era of industrial production, and later automated methods of production, communications systems and surveillance – will be forced into pitiful enterprise after pitiful enterprise in an exhausting and relentless bid for survival. Macroeconomics might seem unwieldy and incomprehensible, but by Plender's estimation they are also underscored by such fundamental injustices as even a child could grasp.

There is a nihilism to the dynamics of the game. And yet nihilism in a system of injustice and inequality can be equivalent to hope. Criticism, after all, contains the belief that things should and can change. Where Plender demonstrates the machinations of inequality, other artists have gone one step further to confront us with the brutal reality of financial hardship and exploitation. In *Cut Piece*, Yoko Ono sat before a museum audience and invited them to slice away at her clothing with a pair of scissors (see p.45). Performance, which had traditionally resisted the tendency to be packaged or resold, rejects the grip of capitalism in and of itself, but this particular performance also highlights themes of greed, ownership and the porous line that exists between self and other, while the myth of art as creation is subverted through the clear act of destruction. As the performance progresses, Ono starts to resemble the impoverished figure of William Beechey's portrait, her dishevelled clothing an affront to the audience members who have contributed to its creation. Oblique and interpretive, it's a work that nevertheless leaves us feeling uneasy and complicit in the exposure and degradation of another; something that we are all responsible for at one time or another as citizens of a capitalist society.

Similarly, a later work by Turner, incomplete and kept private during his lifetime, goes some way to confirming the radical nature of the artist's politics and solidarity with the working class. *The Fall of Anarchy (?)* c.1833–4 eluded scholars for over a century, with its vision of mortality (a cadaver flung over the back of a horse), and was variously, and somewhat unsatisfactorily, considered either a depressive response to his father's death in 1829, or else a meditation on the cholera epidemic of 1832 (see p.46). More recent scholarship, led by art historian Sam Smiles, and building on the observation that the image is incongruous with most biblical and folkloric depictions of death, provides a reading of the painting as a response to Percy Bysshe Shelley's poem, 'The Masque of Anarchy'. Drafted in the wake of the Peterloo Massacre, in which eighteen people died while protesting for manhood suffrage and the right for working-class people to vote on policies shaping their fate after being plunged into poverty by the economic decline following the Napoleonic wars, the poem, which famously ends with the rallying cry, 'Ye are many – they are few!', personifies anarchy thus:

> ... he rode
> On a white horse, splashed with
> blood;
> He was pale even to the lips,
> Like Death in the Apocalypse.

Knowing this, and viewing the dream-like subject emerging from a haze that dislocates it from time and place, it is hard not to see so many contemporary struggles. In spring 2020 and in response to the killing of George Floyd by an armed police officer in the USA, protests erupted around the world in solidarity with Black people who are chastened, punished and stripped of their basic rights in developed countries around the world. During the London chapter of the protest, mounted police officers charged at a group who had gathered to march on Whitehall, leading to the injury of nineteen-year-old student nurse Jessie Tieti Mawutu. The footage, showing the disturbed horse buttressed with armour and careering towards the crowd as instructed, recalled an image that hangs only a few streets away, in an altogether more tranquil and protected environment – an image with a newly acquired symbolism of state brutality and the imbalance of power experienced by all those who continue to seek equality through dissent. Class after all being inextricable from the oppressions of race and colonialism, and the subjects and masters created therein, an echo could be heard from those who had borne witness to similar injustices two centuries earlier and, in the telling, tried to do their part.

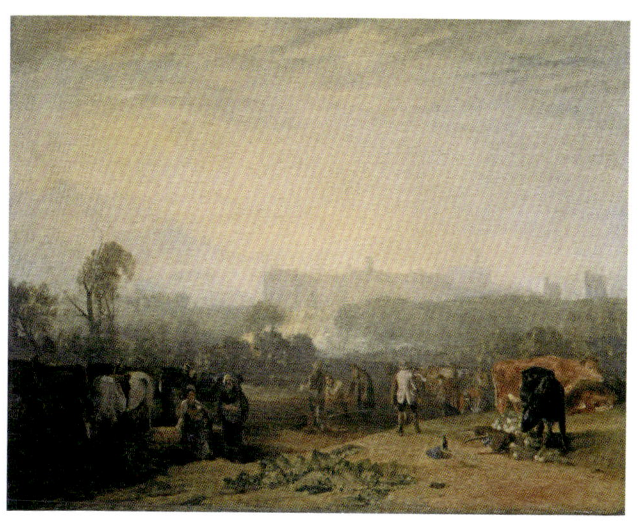

J.M.W. Turner, *Ploughing Up Turnips, near Slough (Windsor)* 1809, oil paint on canvas, 101.9 x 230, Tate

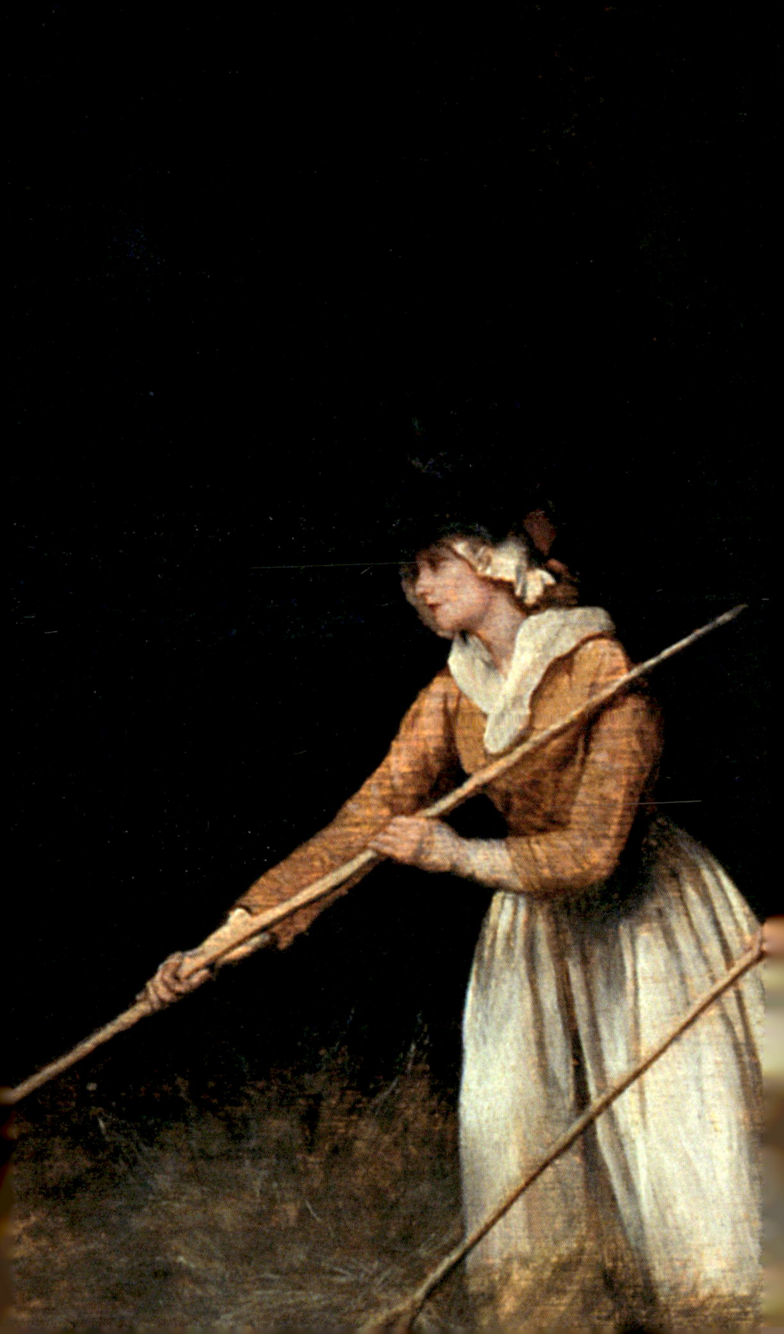

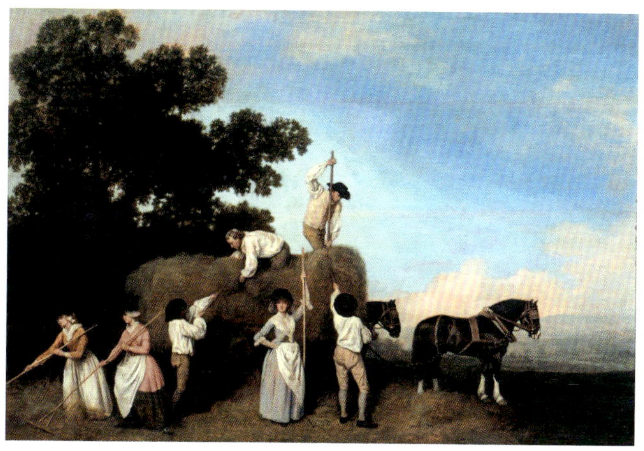

George Stubbs, *Haymakers* 1785, oil paint on wood, 89.5 × 135.3, Tate

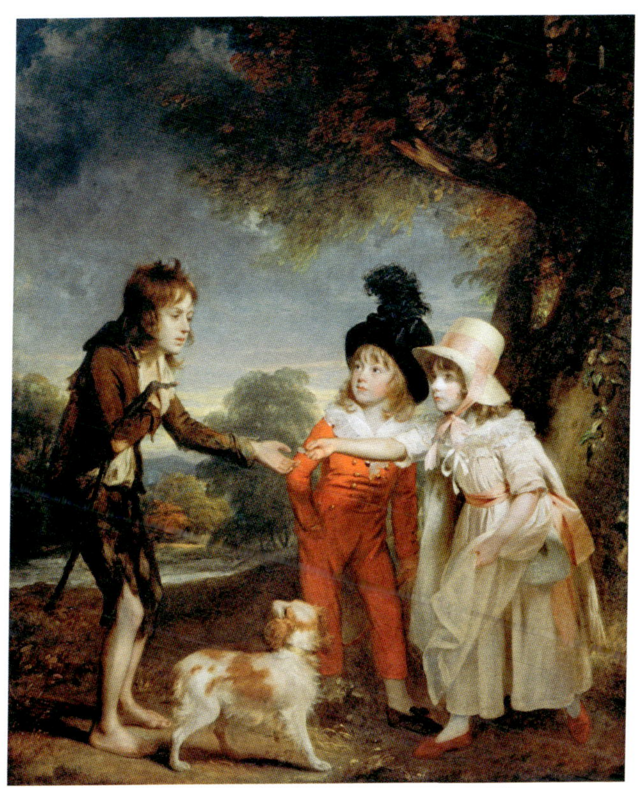

Sir William Beechey, *Portrait of Sir Francis Ford's Children Giving a Coin to a Beggar Boy* 1780, oil paint on canvas, 234.9 × 148.6, Tate

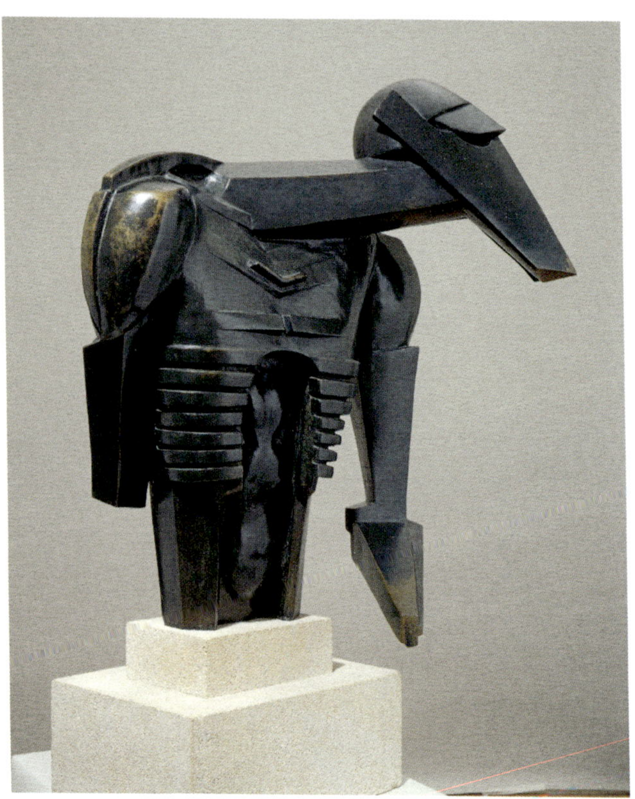

Jacob Epstein, *Torso in Metal from 'The Rock Drill'* 1913–15, bronze,
70.5 × 58.4 × 44.5, Tate

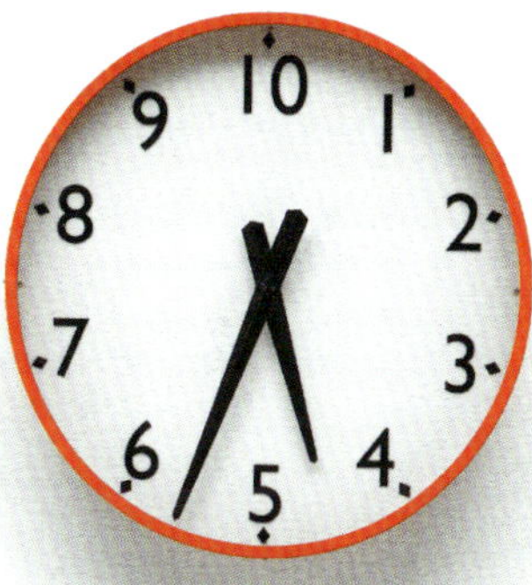

Ruth Ewan, *We could have been anything we wanted to be (red version)*
2011, modified Analogue Clock, 102 × 102 × 30.8, Tate

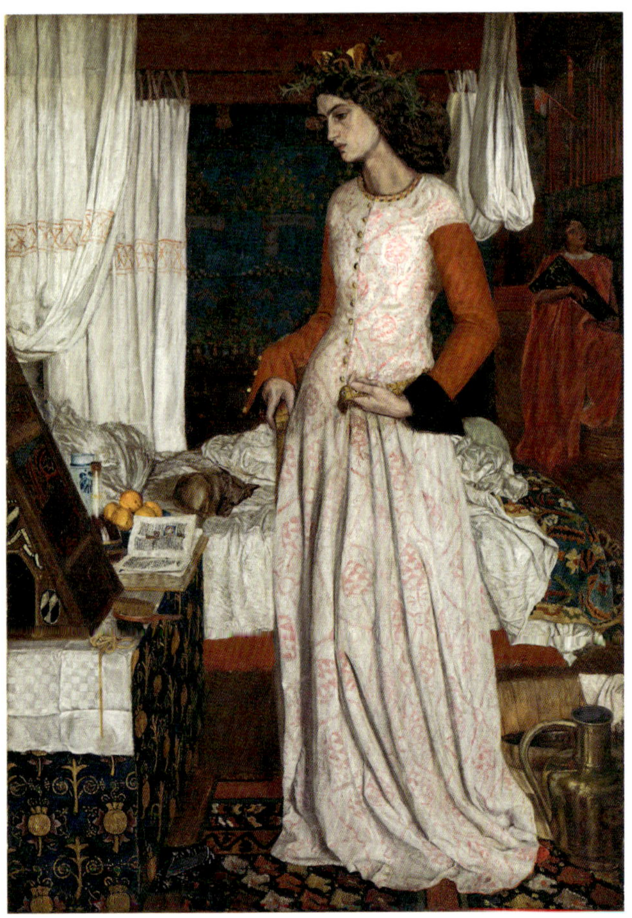

William Morris, *La Belle Iseult* 1858, oil paint on canvas, 71.8 × 50.2, Tate

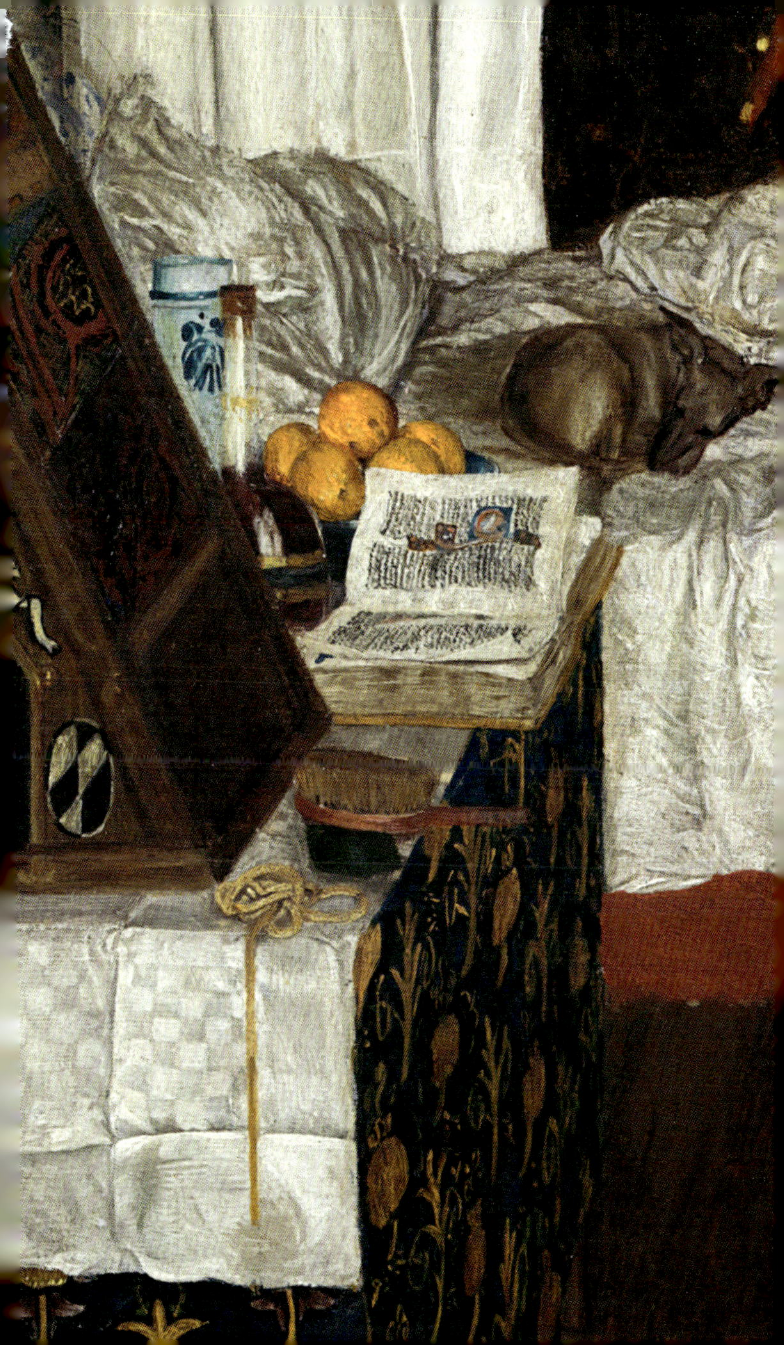

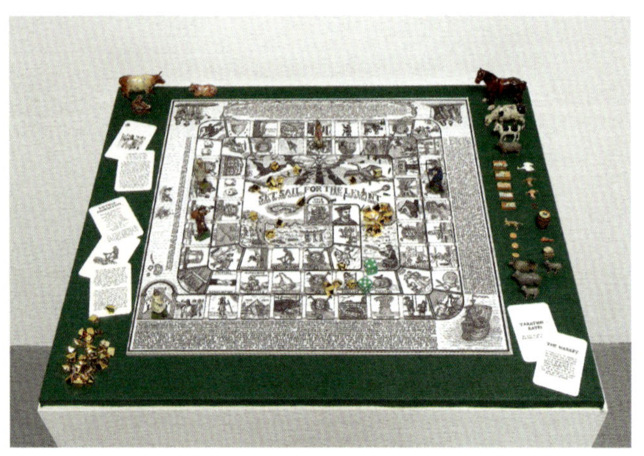

Olivia Plender, *Set Sail for the Levant: A Board Game About Debt (or a social satire)* 2007, ink and correction fluid on paper, 60 digital prints on paper, lead, plastic and dice, dimensions variable, Tate

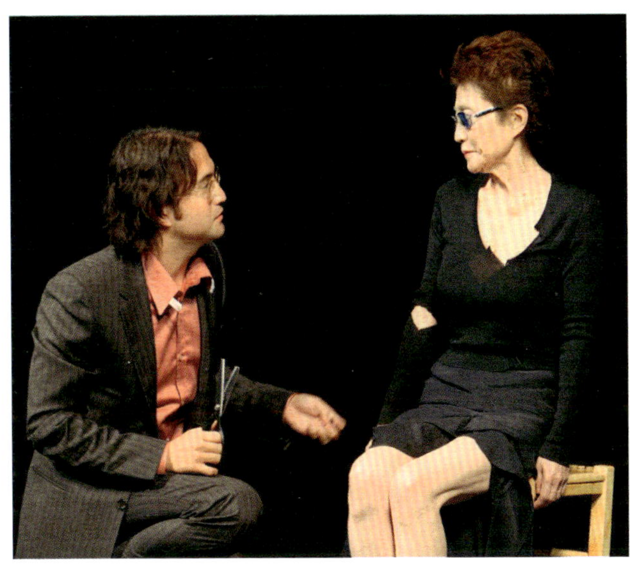

Yoko Ono's son Sean Lennon snips off a piece of his mother's clothing with a pair of scissors during *Cut-Piece*, 15 September 2003, Théâtre le Ranelagh, Paris

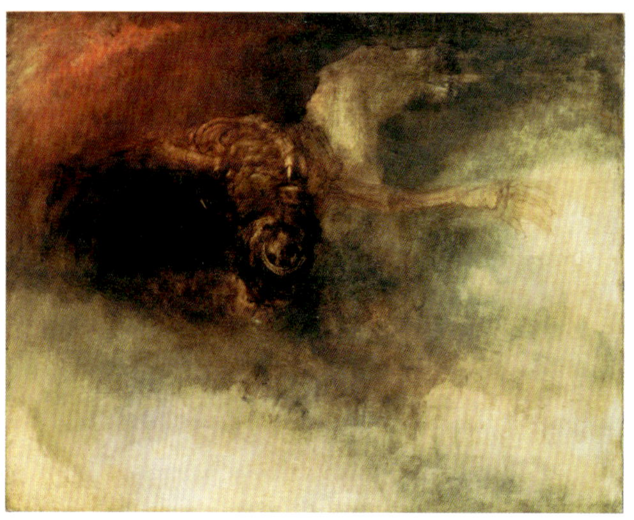

J.M.W. Turner, *The Fall of Anarchy* c.1833–4, oil paint on canvas,
59.7 × 75.6, Tate

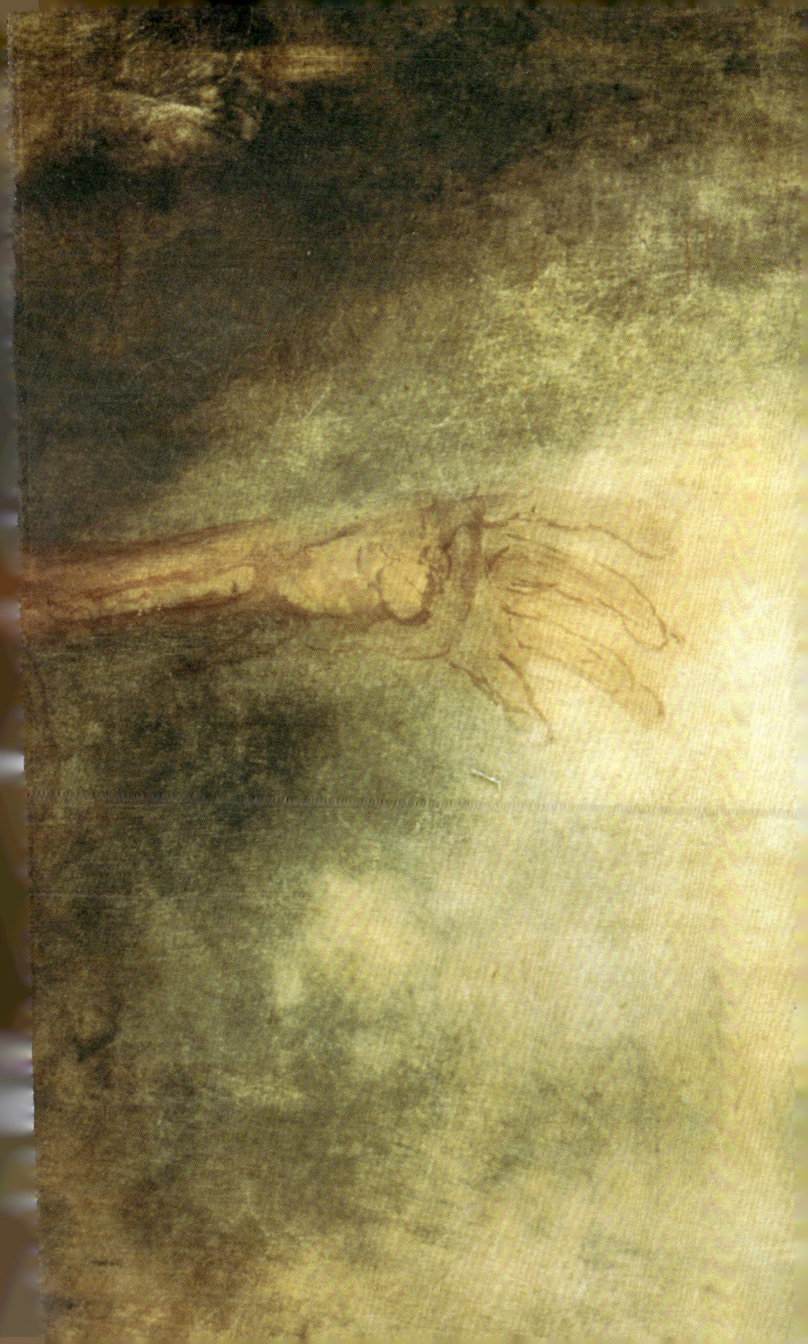